OPRAH WINFREY

Copyright © 2021
University Press
All Rights Reserved

Table of Contents

Introduction
Chapter 1: Early Life
Chapter 2: A Star is Born
Chapter 3: Controversies
Chapter 4: In the Movies
Chapter 5: The Writer
Chapter 6: Romance
Chapter 7: The Philanthropist
Chapter 8: Legacy

Introduction

"My idea of heaven is a great big baked potato and someone to share it with."

Talk show host. Actress. Television producer. Author. Philanthropist. North America's first black multi-billionaire. There cannot be many people on the planet who have not heard of Oprah Winfrey, the woman who was born to a poor, single mother and grew up to be a media powerhouse and the wealthiest African-American of the 20th century.

Winfrey has received numerous awards and accolades throughout her glittering career, including Daytime Emmy Awards, Primetime Emmy Awards, a Tony Award, a Peabody Award, an Academy Award (as well as two additional Oscar nominations), and the Bob Hope Humanitarian Award. She also holds honorary doctorate degrees from Duke and Harvard. In addition, Barak Obama awarded her the Presidential Medal of Freedom. (Her support of Obama is estimated to have won the former president an impressive one million votes during the 2008 Democratic primaries.)

She is credited with revolutionizing the tabloid talk show genre, creating a more confessional format. *The Oprah Winfrey Show* was the highest-rated television program of its kind. Broadcast from Chicago, it had an impressive 25-year run in national syndication from 1986 to 2011, making the so-called 'Queen of All Media' one of the most influential women in the world.

As any other major figure, Winfrey has received more than her fair share of criticism. Having started out with a straightforward talk show format, by the mid-1990s, *The Oprah Winfrey Show* had evolved into a program that focused on self-improvement, spirituality, mindfulness, and literature. Some of the techniques and people she promoted were controversial, such as Dr. Oz, giving rise to a backlash against Winfrey.

In this book, we will examine Winfrey's life and look at how this extraordinary woman was able to rise from humble beginnings to become one of the most powerful African-Americans on the planet.

Chapter 1

Early Life

"The great courageous act that we must all do, is to have the courage to step out of our history and past so that we can live our dreams."

Oprah Gail Winfrey was born in Kosciusko, Mississippi, on January 29, 1954. Named after Ruth's sister-in-law, who is mentioned in the Bible, people regularly mispronounced her name, and eventually, everyone was calling Winfrey Oprah.

Winfrey's mother, Vernita Lee (1935-2018), was 18 when she gave birth to her daughter. Working as a housemaid at the time, she was unmarried, which later gave rise to questions over Winfrey's paternity. The man Winfrey calls 'Dad' was Vernon Winfrey, who had been serving in the armed forces when she was born. However, in 2010, another World War II Veteran, Noah Robinson Sr., came forward with claims that he was her biological father.

According to Winfrey, Robinson was not the first to claim to be her father. During a talk she gave at The New York Women in Communications Matrix Awards, she said, "New daddies are saying 'Hello daughter, call me, I need a new roof.'" Robinson, however, is perhaps the most credible and has stressed that he does not want any money from his alleged daughter and would be more than happy to undergo a DNA test to prove his claims. To date, Winfrey has always refused to carry out a DNA test to prove her paternity, although she did take a test back in 2006, which showed that genetically, she was 89% Sub-Saharan African, 8% Native American, and 3% East Asian, although there is a possibility that the Asian markers may in fact also be Native American.

After Winfrey was born, her mother traveled north searching for work, leaving Winfrey to spend the first six years of her life living rurally with her maternal grandmother, Hattie Mae Lee (1900-1963). Hattie Mae was so poor that Winfrey was frequently forced to wear dresses crafted from potato sacks, making her the target of bullies. A bright child, Winfrey's grandmother taught her to read before she turned three. They were regular attendees at the local church, where Winfrey was dubbed 'The Preacher' for her uncanny ability to memorize Bible verses.

Hattie Mae was apparently abusive and a strict disciplinarian, but the faith that she instilled in her young granddaughter was a gift that sustained her through the worse that was to come. When she was six, Winfrey returned to live with her mother, who was working as a maid, in an inner-city neighborhood in Milwaukee. The long hours took their toll on Lee, who was far less supportive and encouraging to her daughter than Hattie Mae had been. Lee had also given birth to another daughter, Patricia, Winfrey's half-sister. (Patricia would die young at the age of 43 of causes related to cocaine addiction.)

Oprah later recalled what it was like returning home to live with her mother. On the very first night, she was told she would not be allowed to sleep in the house, let alone with her mother. Instead, she was banished to the foyer outside the house. It did not take long for her to realize that this was all to do with her appearance. As Winfrey later put it, "My mother was boarding with this very light-skinned black woman who could have passed for white... I could tell instantly when I walked in the room that she didn't like me. It was because of the color of my skin." This same housemate had a very positive relationship with the lighter-skinned Patricia, which would have compounded Winfrey's feelings of alienation.

By 1962, Lee was struggling to raise both daughters, so the then 12-year-old Winfrey went to live temporarily with her father, who was in Nashville, Tennessee. While Winfrey was away, Lee had a third daughter, whom she placed for adoption due to financial problems. Coincidentally, this child was later called Patricia, but Winfrey was unaware that she had another half-sister until 2010.

This was one of the more secure periods of Winfrey's childhood, and she started to give speeches at social gatherings and church. On one particularly memorable occasion, she was paid $500 for a speech. She later said that was the moment she knew she wanted to be "paid to talk." However, finding Vernon to be too much of a strict disciplinarian, Winfrey moved back in with her mother, who had another baby, Jeffrey. (Jeffrey later died of AIDS-related complications in 1989.) Unfortunately, things would go rapidly downhill for Winfrey.

In later life, Winfrey was very open about how abusive her childhood had been. During an interview with David Letterman in 2012, she talked about how she was regularly beaten and described one particularly notable occasion while she was living with her grandmother. She had been sent to get some water from a well and carry it back in a bucket. She played with the water with her fingers, a natural child's play, but when her grandmother saw her, she beat her so badly that she left Winfrey with welts on her back. These welts bled for a while, so when she put on her Sunday dress, Winfrey got blood on the dress, resulting in another beating for spoiling her clothes.

However, the most horrific story first came out during a 1986 episode of *The Oprah Winfrey Show,* focusing on sexual abuse. Winfrey said that while her mother was working, she was left in the care of her cousin, uncle, and a family friend, whom all molested her. At the age of 9, she was raped. Winfrey went on to give the heart-breaking detail that afterwards, "He took me to an ice cream shop — blood still running down my leg — and bought me ice cream." When Winfrey finally discussed the alleged abuse with her family when she was 24, they allegedly refused to believe her.

Winfrey was abused between the ages of nine to fourteen when she discovered she was pregnant. Her mother had enough of dealing with the teenager and tried to place her in a detention home, but it was full. Lee told her daughter, "you are getting your ass out of this house," so Oprah was sent back to her father, who banned her from dating, unaware that she was already pregnant.

Winfrey gave birth to a premature son who died when he was just two weeks old. Winfrey kept the details about her son private, but in 1990, one of her family members sold the story to the *National Enquirer.* Winfrey later wrote about the experience in *O, The Oprah Magazine,* in which she did not name the relative, but described how they "sat in a room, told them the story of my hidden shame and left their offices $19,000 richer." The Associated Press revealed that the source was Winfrey's half-sister, Patricia Lloyd.

Initially, Winfrey said that she cried for three days over the pain of being betrayed by her family and worried that the news would damage her career. The reality was, "No one said a word … not strangers, not even people I knew. I was shocked. Nobody treated me differently. For 20 years, I had been expecting a reaction that never came. And, I soon realized that having the secret out was liberating... What I learned for sure was that holding the shame was the greatest burden of all."

When her son died, both Winfrey and her father took this as an opportunity to start afresh. In Oprah's words, "I really felt like that baby's life — that baby coming into the world — really gave me new life. That's how I processed it for myself."

Vernon prioritized Winfrey's education, and she became an honors student, coming second in the nation in dramatic interpretation. Winfrey went on to win an oratory contest, which enabled her to secure a full scholarship to Tennessee State University, where she studied communication. During her senior year of high school and in her first two years of college, Winfrey did the news part-time at a local black radio station, WVOL. She was offered a job reading the afternoon headlines after winning Nashville's Miss Fire Prevention contest, which WVOL sponsored.

Winfrey was making her first steps towards building the media career that would transform her into a household name. While her time with her grandmother may not always have been a happy one, Winfrey later gave credit to Hattie Mae for supporting her to pursue a life in the spotlight, saying that it was her grandmother who had encouraged her to speak in public and "gave me a positive sense of myself."

Chapter 2

A Star is Born

"You don't become what you want, you become what you believe."

Winfrey quickly recognized her talents, becoming both the youngest news anchor and the first black female news anchor at Nashville's WLAC-TV (now WTVF-TV). In 1976, she accepted a co-anchor position for Baltimore's WJZ-TV's six o'clock news, although, in 1977, she was demoted from co-anchor and side-lined to lower-profile positions. This setback did not deter Winfrey, however, who was soon signed up to co-host with Richard Sher on WJZ's local talk show, *People Are Talking,* as well as hosting the local version of *Dialing for Dollars.*

In 1983, Winfrey relocated to Chicago, a move that would prove to be truly life-changing. She was hired to host WLS-TV's poorly performing half-hour morning talk show, *A.M. Chicago,* which premiered on January 2, 1984. Within months of Winfrey taking the helm, the show leapfrogged from having the worst rankings to outperform *Donahue* as the highest-rated talk show in Chicago. Her surprising success led to movie critic, Roger Ebert, approaching her to sign a syndication deal with King World. It has been reported that, while on the first of two dates between Ebert and Winfrey in the mid-1980s, Ebert wrote some numbers on a napkin while they were out at a restaurant. He felt that she would attract 40 times the revenue that his own show, *At the Movies,* was making. He passed the napkin over to Oprah, who, when she saw the figures in question, said, "Deal done!"

A.M. Chicago has rebranded *The Oprah Winfrey Show* and went from a half-hour slot to a full hour of talk. The first episode was broadcast to the nation on September 8, 1986. Not only did Winfrey overtake Donahue in the Chicago ratings, but her newly syndicated show also dethroned Donahue as the number-one daytime talk show in America, bringing in double his national audience.

Oprah had wanted Don Johnson to appear on the first national episode of her show. The actor was starring in *Miami Vice,* the biggest show on TV at the time, and his appearance would have been a real draw to viewers. She even sent him a pair of expensive rhinestone sunglasses in a bid to persuade him to come on the show, but the bribe was not enough, and Johnson turned her down. It is possible that this was the making of *The Oprah Winfrey Show* because Oprah decided against finding an alternative star, instead deciding to make the show about ordinary people as well as celebrities. She and her team came up with the concept 'How to Marry the Man of Your Choice' and the idea proved to be a hit. Johnson eventually appeared on the first episode of the show's final season in 2010, almost 25 years after he had first been approached. (And he even returned the sunglasses!)

Unsurprisingly, Winfrey's meteoric rise was the subject of much discussion in the press. *TIME* magazine ruminated that Winfrey went against all expectations of the ideal talk show host: "Few people would have bet on Oprah Winfrey's swift rise to host the most popular talk show on TV. In a field dominated by white males, she is a black female of ample bulk."

Other commentators remarked on Winfrey's humor, compassion, and empathy. Winfrey seemed genuinely moved by her guests' stories, even crying at times, which encouraged her guests to go more in-depth into their stories than they might otherwise have intended. Winfrey fostered an atmosphere of cozy intimacy, one which was akin to group therapy, encouraging the subject to open up and be vulnerable. *Newsday* stated that Winfrey was "far better attuned to her audience, if not the world [than Donahue]" and it was perhaps this down-to-earth, girl next door approach that was the key to Winfrey's success.

Initially, *The Oprah Winfrey Show* was classed as a tabloid talk show, but as time wore on, the emphasis slowly shifted, and by the mid-1990s, Winfrey was branching out to do shows on issues such as geopolitics, health, and spirituality. When she interviewed celebrities, she delved into the social issues they were passionate about, such as their charity work or personal experiences with substance abuse, and hosted televised giveaways, giving rise to memorable moments and catchphrases like "You get a car! You get a car! You get a car!"

However, this change was not without times of controversy. For example, Ellen DeGeneres decided to come out as a lesbian on *The Oprah Winfrey Show* in 1997, an event which was mirrored on her sitcom. Winfrey was cast as Ellen's therapist on *Ellen,* which featured Ellen's character coming out. Winfrey later revealed that she had received a lot of backlashes. In a 2013 episode of *Oprah's Next Chapter,* she said. "I played the therapist on that show... and got the most and worst hate mail of my entire career after doing it, like 'Go back to Africa' hate mail."

That was not the only impact of Winfrey appearing on *Ellen.* Rumors began circulating that she and best friend Gayle King were a lesbian couple. The rumors persisted for years until Winfrey finally addressed the issue in the August 2006 issue of *O* magazine. She wrote, "I understand why people think we're gay. There isn't a definition in our culture for this kind of bond between women. So I get why people have to label it—how can you be this close without it being sexual? I've told nearly everything there is to tell. All my stuff is out there. People think I'd be so ashamed of being gay that I wouldn't admit it? Oh, please."

Over the years, there were many, many highlight moments on *The Oprah Winfrey Show.* Winfrey was known for having weight issues, with her weight fluctuating massively over the years. In one early episode, following a much-publicized diet, Winfrey came out on stage pulling a wagon piled high with 67 pounds of animal fat to show how much weight she had lost. Winfrey later stated that she regretted the stunt, telling *Entertainment Tonight,* "Big, big, big, big, big, big, big mistake! When I look at that show, I think it was one of the biggest ego trips of my life."

Winfrey was also responsible for hosting the most-watched interview in history (and the fourth most-watched event on American TV) when she sat down with Michael Jackson in 1993. Filmed at his home, the Neverland Ranch, it was the performer's first interview in almost 15 years. Naturally, the King of Pop was a source of fascination for many viewers, and an incredible 90 million people worldwide tuned in to see the interview, which was carried out before Jackson became the target of allegations of sexual abuse.

Winfrey's personal touch continued to be a feature of the show, and in 1995, Winfrey admitted on-air that she had smoked cracked cocaine during her 20s. She was interviewing four mothers who were recovering drug addicts, with *Washington Post* journalist Patrice Gaines joining her as co-host. During the discussion, Winfrey confessed, "Let me say this, and this is probably one of the hardest things I've ever said, but I was involved with a man in my 20s who introduced me to the same drug that you've been talking about and, like Patrice, I always felt that the drug itself is not the problem but that I was addicted to the man. I can't think of anything I wouldn't have done for that man."

In 1996, Winfrey launched the Oprah's Book Club segment on her show. The feature proved to be popular and a testament to how powerful the Oprah seal of approval can go. Every book announced as the next read in the club went on to become a best-seller, giving rise to the term 'The Oprah Effect.'

She co-founded the women's cable television network, Oxygen, which initially aired her *Oprah After the Show* program, which ran from 2002-06, when it was moved to Oprah.com following Winfrey's sale of her share in the network. She continues to be the president of her film and television production company, Harpo Productions, which is her name spelled backwards and the name of the man her character married in *The Color Purple.* Not only was Harpo Productions responsible for *The Oprah Winfrey Show, but* it also produced many other successful shows, such as *Rachael Ray, The Dr. Oz Show,* and *Dr. Phil.*

On January 15, 2008, Winfrey joined forces with Discovery Communications and announced that Discovery Health Channel would be rebranded as OWN: Oprah Winfrey Network. OWN was initially supposed to launch in 2009, but delays meant that it did not go live until January 1, 2011, which was also the year that saw the very last episode of *The Oprah Winfrey Show.*

While Oprah's eponymous show might have ended, she continued to host, and in September 2017, she joined the CBS show *60 Minutes* as a special contributor to the Sunday evening news discussion show. She appeared on the show until late 2018.

In June 2018, Apple announced that it had signed a content partnership with Winfrey to run for several years and would see her creating original, new programs exclusive to Apple TV+. The first show, *Oprah's Book Club,* aired on November 1, 2019, and was inspired by the popular segment of the same name from her old talk show. A second show, *Oprah Talks Covid-19,* debuted on March 21, 2020, as a response to the Covid-19 pandemic, while a third show,

The Oprah Conversation, debuted in July of the same year. It saw Winfrey sitting down with "foremost newsmakers, thought leaders, and masters of their craft" for in-depth discussions about the pressing issues of the day.

Chapter 3

Controversies

"Self-esteem comes from being able to define the world in your own terms and refusing to abide by the judgments of others."

While *The Oprah Winfrey Show* was hugely popular, it was not without its fair share of criticism and controversy, especially in later years, when Winfrey was censured for allowing celebrities to share pseudoscientific claims on her show, such as Suzanne Somers' support for bioidenticals and Jenny McCarthy's attitude towards vaccines. Many critics felt that Winfrey was too easy when interviewing celebrities and politicians with whom she felt a personal affinity with when she should be more aggressive and pose challenging follow-up questions and allow her personal bias to affect whom she booked as a guest. For example, in September 2008, Matt Drudge of the *Drudge Report* said that Winfrey had refused to host Sarah Palin on her show, allegedly out of loyalty towards Barack Obama, whom Winfrey publicly supported. Winfrey denied the claim, saying that Palin's appearance had never been discussed, and having come out in support of Obama, she had made a decision not to allow her show to be used as a platform for *any* candidate. While Obama had made two appearances on her show, this was before his candidacy. Winfrey also said that she felt that Palin would be an excellent guest and would be more than happy to welcome her on the show once the election was over, which duly happened on November 18, 2009.

In 2006, rappers Ice Cube, 50 Cent, and Ludacris collectively spoke out against Winfrey for a perceived anti-hip-hop bias on her part. Talking to *GQ* magazine, Ludacris stated that Winfrey was hard on him about his lyrics and edited some of the comments he had made while appearing on her show with cast members from the film *Crash*. In fact, Ludacris claimed that he was not even invited initially to appear on the show with his fellow cast members.

Winfrey's explained that she respected hip artists but took issue with rap lyrics that "marginalize women." She also pointed out that she had spoken to Ludacris following his appearance to explain her stance and told him that while she understood his music was meant as entertainment, some of his listeners might take it literally.

With the Oprah Effect guaranteeing success for any author lucky enough to be selected for her book club, many vied for acceptance. One chosen author, James Frey, had his book featured in 2006. *A Million Little Pieces* was touted as a 'brutally honest' memoir about his alcohol and drug addiction recovery. Winfrey announced it by saying, "If you've ever had to live through this with somebody you love, here is a story that was written for you," going on to feature a number of extracts from Frey's book. Frey's account included stories about how he had woken up on an airplane with no memory of how he had got there – nor how he had lost his teeth; his subsequent dental surgery without anesthesia; what it was like to freebase cocaine and snort glue.

According to the New York Times, Winfrey's positive endorsement of *A Million Little Pieces* helped Frey sell over 2 million copies in the following two months.

There was only one problem: Frey had made up much of the book.

Journalists began to research Frey's claims, and the reality was very different from Frey's experiences. For example, in one anecdote, Frey discussed getting high before getting behind the wheel of a car and driving into a police officer. He then got into a fight with the officer and ended up spending three months in jail. He had simply run his tire over a curb and paid bail for driving under the influence. In another instance, he claimed that he had been blamed for a teenager's fatal car accident, but when *The Post* reached out to the girls' parents, they said they had no knowledge of this.

Frey was forced to admit that he had exaggerated much of what he had written about, but Winfrey continued to stand by him. In an interview with Larry King, she said, "What is relevant is that he was a drug addict who spent years in turmoil. It seems to be much ado about nothing."

Winfrey's support for Frey saw the critics turn on her too, with the *Washington Post* calling her 'deluded.' After a few days of merciless criticism by the press, Winfrey brought Frey back on to her show and tore him to pieces. In one particularly difficult moment, she said to the author, "You conned us all. That's a lie. It's not an idea, James. That's a lie."

That was not the end of the matter. The following year, Winfrey appeared on King's show again to deny that she had mistreated the author she had previously supported. As a result, in 2011, over five years after Frey's initial appearance on her show, Winfrey invited him to appear yet again and publicly apologized for her "lack of compassion."

Cynics observed that Frey had a new book coming out he wanted to plug at the time of this final interview.

Oprah famously became embroiled in a lawsuit with a group of Texan ranchers following an episode of *The Oprah Winfrey Show* in 1996. Broadcast a few years after the peak of the so-called 'Mad Cow Disease', there were some who were still nervous about consuming beef products out of fear of catching the potentially fatal illness. Their fears were not allayed when Winfrey invited a vegetarian activist onto her show.

During their interview, Winfrey asked the activist whether they had said that Mad Cow Disease "could make AIDS look like the common cold." When they replied, "Absolutely," Winfrey immediately said, "It has just stopped me from eating another burger!"

According to ranchers, beef prices tumbled to an incredible 10-year-low the next day.

As a result of this fall in prices, a group of ranchers collectively sued Winfrey under a Texas law prohibiting any from making "disparaging statements about perishable food products." They argued that Oprah's comments had been directly responsible for the fall in cattle prices, costing beef farmers $11 million. A judge downgraded the case to a defamation suit, but Winfrey had to relocate her show to Amarillo while she dealt with the allegations.

Fans crowded the street in front of the courtroom during the 1998 trial, in which a jury finally determined that there was no case to answer since Winfrey had not intended to undermine the beef industry. Upon hearing the news, fans toasted the result with champagne outside the courthouse while Winfrey reiterated her resolve never to eat another burger. She said, "Free speech not only lives, it rocks, [and] I'm still off hamburgers."

However, the beef industry continued to be disgruntled with Winfrey, and *Beef Magazine* published an op-ed piece called "Why Does Oprah Continue to Bully Beef?" in which it discussed Winfrey's attack on factory farms in her magazine.

One interesting consequence of the trial was the launch of Phil McGraw's television career. During preparation for the trial, Oprah hired McGraw and his firm of legal consultants, Courtroom Sciences, Inc. They were tasked with analyzing the jury, and Winfrey was so impressed with McGraw's work that she invited him on her show, making the Texan cattle farmers indirectly responsible for *Dr. Phil.*

Another television personality who can thank Winfrey for his career is "America's doctor," Mehmet Oz. Dr. Oz appeared on *The Oprah Winfrey Show* in the mid-2000s to give health advice, covering such vital subjects as 'Everybody Poops.' He appeared on the show more than 60 times before Harpo Productions gave him his own show, *The Dr. Oz Show.* Potentially America's most influential physician, Dr. Oz, is a controversial figure for his support of alternative medicine, including homeopathy. In fact, Dr. Oz was awarded the James Randi Educational Foundation's Pigasus Award from 2009 to 2012 as a consequence of his promotion of energy therapies and faith healing, as well as his support of communication with the dead and "quack medical practices, paranormal belief, and pseudoscience."

A 2014 study published in the *British Medical Journal* discovered that medical talk shows such as *The Dr. Oz Show* frequently failed to give appropriate information on the specific benefits or evidence of their claims. Forty episodes of the program from early 2013 were evaluated, as were the same number of episodes of *The Doctors.* This analysis found that current evidence supported 46%, contradicted 15%, and could not be sourced for 39% of the recommendations made on *The Dr. Oz Show.*

Although Oprah stood beside Dr. Oz throughout his many controversies, he was eventually dropped by her network.

Dr. Oz's advice was not the only health-related controversy associated with *The Oprah Winfrey Show.* After she did a feature on *The Secret,* breast cancer sufferer, Kim Tinkham decided to heal herself.

The Secret is problematic in many circles because it claims that emotional, financial, and health issues can be cured through thinking positive thoughts, and there are many books and DVDs available to purchase to help individuals see the benefits for themselves.

Having discovered *The Secret* through *The Oprah Winfrey Show*, Tinkham told Winfrey in 2007 that the system had given her the confidence to ignore the advice of her doctors, who had said she needed immediate surgery and treatment. Instead, Tinkham intended to think her way back to good health.

While Winfrey still supported the concepts promoted in *The Secret,* she attempted to get Tinkham to change her mind, saying, "I'm really happy the message, or certainly some of the message, is reaching mass consciousness," but suggesting that Tinkham could combine a positive, healing mindset with a partial mastectomy.

Tinkham chose to ignore Winfrey as well as her doctors and sadly passed away three years later.

Chapter 4

In the Movies

"The biggest adventure you can ever take is to live the life of your dreams."

In 1985, Winfrey made her big-screen debut co-starring in Steven Spielberg's adaptation of Alice Walker's novel *The Color Purple.* Winfrey told the story of how she won the role to a rapt audience at Essence Fest in 2016.

Winfrey was a huge fan of the novel, so when she heard that it would be adapted for film, she immediately knew she had to be a part of it, no matter what. Winfrey said, "I started praying to God, 'Please help me find a role in The Color Purple. I didn't need a speaking role. I was willing to carry the script, help people with the water."

At the time, she was the morning news host on *A.M. Chicago,* and it so happened that one of the producers, Quincy Jones, was in Chicago to handle a lawsuit filed against Michael Jackson. Apparently, as he was coming out of the shower in his hotel room, he saw Winfrey on TV and instantly called Reuben Cannon, the casting agent, to tell him that he thought he had found Sophia.

Cannon invited Winfrey along for an audition, but when she did not hear anything for three months, she rang Cannon directly. Cannon was not impressed by her initiative, telling her, "You don't call me. I call you. And I didn't call you. Do you understand I have real actresses who have auditioned for this part?"

Winfrey was devastated, convinced that her weight was the reason for the lack of response. She decided to "go to a fat farm" and lose 25 pounds to improve her chances of winning the role.

Winfrey was going for a run at the health farm, praying to God to help her lose weight. She said, "I keep hearing this noise. There is nobody on the track but me. And I look around, and it's my thighs rubbing together. It's my thighs rubbing together causing this thunderous sound. Then I really start to cry." Deciding that the only way she could release her emotions, Winfrey started singing "I Surrender All," a hymn she remembered fondly from church. She was asking God to let her weight go, asking him to help her go to the movie and bless the actors who had been cast.

In Winfrey's words, "The instant I let it go, a woman comes running out of the cafeteria screaming, 'Ofrey, is your name Ofrey?' Ten years, still no one knew how to pronounce my name. 'Somebody is on the telephone for you, says his name is Spielberg,'"

Winfrey took the call, and sure enough, it was the director. He asked her whether she was at a fat farm, and she corrected him, saying she was at a health retreat. Spielberg told her to come to his office in California, warning her that she might lose the role if she lost so much as a pound.

Winfrey immediately packed her bags and left, stopping at the Dairy Queen for a large ice cream in case she had lost weight during her run. She arrived at Spielberg's office the next day, and he told her she had been hired.

Spielberg's astute casting paid off. Winfrey was nominated for an Academy Award for her performance as Sophia.

In October 1998, Winfrey returned to the big screen when she produced and starred in an adaptation of Toni Morrison's Pulitzer Prize-winning novel, *Beloved.* When she read the book, Winfrey immediately knew she wanted to adapt it for the screen and was desperate to secure the film rights. Unfortunately, it was the weekend, and she had no means of contacting Morrison since she did not have the author's number. Demonstrating typical Winfrey out-of-the-box thinking, she found out which town Morrison lived in and rang the local fire department to ask them to get the author to contact her. Morrison duly did, and Winfrey was able to make the film.

Winfrey played Sethe, a former slave. In preparation for the role, Winfrey participated in a slavery exercise in which she was kidnapped, tied up, blindfolded, and left alone in the woods. She later described the experience as "death with no salvation."

However, the Oprah Effect did not seem to be able to work its magic on *Beloved.* Despite an extensive advertising campaign and no fewer than two episodes of The Oprah Winfrey Show focusing on nothing but the film, Beloved lost around $30 million.

Despite the setback, Winfrey continued to be involved in films, providing the voice for Gussie the goose in Charlotte's Web (2006), Judge Bumbleton in Bee Movie (2007), and Eudora in The Princess and the Frog (2010), as well as providing the voice over for the US version of the BBC nature documentary Life. Meanwhile, in late 2008, Winfrey's company, Harpo Films, signed a deal to produce series, documentaries, and films for HBO.

Chapter 5

The Writer

"Challenges are gifts that force us to search for a new center of gravity. Don't fight them. Just find a new way to stand."

It should come as no surprise that for someone who built a career out of her way with words, not only has Winfrey hosted a talk show, but she has also co-authored several books. One of them, a weight-loss book published in 2005, and co-authored with her personal trainer, Bob Greene, has smashed records for the world's largest book advance fee, an honor previously held by former US President Bill Clinton for his autobiography.

In 2015, Winfrey's memoir, *The Life You Want,* was announced after her tour. The book was supposed to be published in 2017, but in 2016 it was reported that the autobiography had been "indefinitely postponed."

Winfrey is also behind *O, The Oprah Magazine,* and for four years (2004-2008), also published a second magazine called *O At Home.* In 2002, *Fortune* described *O, The Oprah Magazine,* as the most successful start-up ever in the magazine industry. While *The Oprah Winfrey Show* was targeted at the average woman in the street, Winfrey's magazine readers are from a higher demographic, with the average reader earning more than the median for US women.

However, in July 2020, it was announced that *O Magazine* would no longer be printed after December of that year, instead shifting to a digital model. Winfrey thanked readers in the final edition, although she did leave the door open for potential one-off publications by saying that this was the "final monthly print edition."

Instead, Winfrey focused more on her website, Oprah.com, an unsurprising move since magazines. In addition, the impact of the Covid-19 pandemic has also hit print advertising revenue, with research firm Magna predicting in June 2020 that US national magazines would see an incredible drop of 23%.

Oprah.com receives an average of 70 million+ page views per month from over six million users. In comparison, the Alliance for Audited Media reported that the print magazine had a total circulation of just 2.3 million in the last six months of 2019. Initially set up to provide additional resources and content linked to Winfrey's shows, magazines, book club, and charity, Oprah.com offers Winfrey the opportunity to promote causes and issues she feels passionate about. For example, Winfrey set up "Oprah's Child Predator Watch List" on the site in a bid to find accused child molesters. Just 48 hours after the list first went live, two of the featured men had been caught.

Chapter 6

Romance

"The chance to love and be loved exists no matter where you are."

Although Winfrey went through a wild phase when she was a teenager, she did have one stable relationship with her high school sweetheart, Anthony Otey. The pair went to prom together and were voted the most popular students at East Nashville High School in 1971. Otey still has hundreds of letters Oprah wrote to him during their courtship and has said that Winfrey was a model student who behaved with dignity. While they discussed marriage, Otey claims that he always had a feeling that Oprah was destined for more extraordinary things than he could ever achieve, which meant that when she broke up with him on Valentine's Day of her senior year, it was not entirely a surprise.

Several months later, Winfrey met William 'Bubba' Taylor at Tennessee State University.

CBS journalist George Mair claimed that Taylor was Winfrey's "first intense, to die for love affair." Winfrey supported Taylor to get a job at WVOL and subsequently said, "We really did care for each other, " Winfrey would later recall. "We shared a deep love. A love I will never forget." However, when she moved to Baltimore in 1976 to work at WJZ-TV, Taylor chose to stay in Nashville, despite her doing all she could to persuade him not to break up with her, "including literally begging him on her knees to stay with her" according to Mair. Winfrey was unsuccessful, and the couple split up.

Winfrey had many relationships after breaking up with Taylor, such as dating John Tesh, a former *Entertainment Tonight* co-host. Tesh later revealed that 'Oprah and I were cub reporters in Nashville nearly 40 years ago, and we dated for a short time." Winfrey's biographer Kitty Kelley alleged that Tesh left Winfrey because he could not handle the pressure of being in an interracial relationship, although the two remained friends.

When Winfrey was going through a tough time at WJZ-TV, reporter Lloyd Kramer was there to dry her eyes. Management criticized Winfrey for crying on air while reporting on tragic stories and had issues with her appearance, especially when her hair fell out after a poorly done perm. Winfrey spoke fondly of Kramer in later years, saying, "Lloyd was just the best. That man loved me even when I was bald! He was wonderful. He stuck with me through the whole demoralizing experience. That man was the most fun romance I ever had."

After Kramer moved to join NBC in New York, Winfrey fell into an unhealthier relationship. According to Mair, she started seeing a married man who refused to leave his wife. The man's identity has never been revealed, but Winfrey has said of him, "I'd had a relationship with a man for four years. I wasn't living with him. I'd never lived with anyone—and I thought I was worthless without him. The more he rejected me, the more I wanted him. I felt depleted, powerless. At the end, I was down on the floor on my knees groveling and pleading with him".

On September 8, 1981, things got so bad that she wrote a suicide note to her best friend Gayle King asking her to water her plants. Winfrey later downplayed the intentions behind the note because "I couldn't kill myself. I would be afraid the minute I did it, something really good would happen, and I'd miss it."

As it was, the stress of the relationship took its toll, and Winfrey believes that it played a prominent role in her issues with weight. "The reason I gained so much weight in the first place and the reason I had such a sorry history of abusive relationships with men was I just needed approval so much. I needed everyone to like me because I didn't like myself much. So I'd end up with these cruel self-absorbed guys who'd tell me how selfish I was, and I'd say 'Oh thank you, you're so right' and be grateful to them. Because I had no sense that I deserved anything else. Which is also why I gained so much weight later on. It was the perfect way of cushioning myself against the world's disapproval."

When she met Stedman Graham at a charity event held in Chicago in 1986, all that changed. Writing in *O Mag's* February 2020 issue, Winfrey said that she had seen Graham around town, but he was in a relationship, so she thought nothing would come of it. Then, one day, they were both at a sick friend's house. Graham was now single, and as they left, Winfrey asked him if he wanted to go and get a beer. "He said he didn't drink. (Still doesn't—not one sip of nothin' alcoholic since I've known him). I thought he was nice enough, but I wasn't that impressed. He was polite, yes, and kind. The sort of guy who sits with an ailing friend. Tall and handsome, for sure. But actually too handsome, I thought, to be interested in me."

Graham was most definitely interested, and the couple began seeing each other, starting a romance that was to endure. In an episode of *The Oprah Winfrey Show* filmed in November 1988, Winfrey referred to Graham when discussing her weight loss, saying, "I love Stedman very much. And he cares about me and has been very supportive of me, fat and thin. I did not do this for Stedman...You know you cannot [lose weight] for anybody but yourself." However, in 2011, Winfrey admitted that part of the motivation for losing weight was a need to match up to Graham's physical standards. She felt self-conscious when they were together and believed that people seeing them together would wonder why he was with "that fat girl."

Despite rumors of infidelity, the couple stayed together, and after they had been seeing each other for six years, they announced their engagement in a 1992 *People* cover story. The couple had been living together since 1991, and Graham, who had been married before, came home and told Winfrey, "I want you to marry me. I think it's time." In fact, despite setting a date for

1993, the couple never did exchange vows and continue to be happy just living together even today.

In 2008, Winfrey spoke to *E! News* about how her and Graham kept their relationship strong. She said, "I happen to be with a man who has always appreciated the fact that I was...considered a powerful person. [He's] not trying to crowd in on it, not competing with it. He knows how to hold his own." A couple of years later, Graham appeared on *The Oprah Winfrey Show* and gave his own perspective. He said, "We want each other to succeed. And I want her to succeed and to be as successful as she possibly can, so I encourage that. That's not always an easy thing to do when you're a man in a relationship with a very powerful woman. So I'm not threatened by her fame or her success or money."

Despite being one of the more enduring Hollywood couples, the question of their having never married has continued to raise questions. In 2017, Winfrey appeared on the cover of *Vogue.* In the accompanying article, she said, "I said to Stedman, 'What would have happened if we had actually gotten married?' And the answer is: 'We wouldn't be together.' We would not have stayed together because marriage requires a different way of being in this world. His interpretation of what it means to be a husband and what it would mean for me to be a wife would have been pretty traditional, and I would not have been able to fit into that."

In the February 2020 edition of *O Mag,* Winfrey expanded upon her reasons for accepting Graham's proposal but never marrying him. "For years, there were hundreds of tabloid stories, weekly, on whether we would marry. In 1993, the moment after I said yes to his proposal, I had doubts. I realized I didn't actually want a marriage. I wanted to be asked. I wanted to know he felt I was worthy of being his missus, but I didn't want the sacrifices, the compromises, the day-in-day-out commitment required to make a marriage work. My life with the show was my priority, and we both knew it."

During the Covid-19 pandemic, Oprah shared touching footage of the couple reuniting following 14 days of self-isolation from each other. The pair seemed delighted to be together again, demonstrating that despite the pressures of being a Hollywood power couple, they seem to have discovered the secret to a successful long-term relationship.

Chapter 7

The Philanthropist

"Doing the best at this moment puts you in the best place for the next moment."

Winfrey has a long history of philanthropy, always happy to share the wealth she has accumulated.

In 1998, Winfrey established the Oprah's Angel Network, a charity supporting charitable projects and giving grants to non-profit organizations internationally. During the charity's existence, Oprah's Angel Network raised over $80,000,000, with Winfrey personally covering all the administration costs to ensure that 100% of all donations raised could go directly to the charity.

In 2005, Oprah set up a sister organization. The Oprah Angel Network Katrina registry was established in response to Hurricane Katrina. The charity raised over $11 million for relief efforts, with Winfrey personally donating $10 million to help local residents. The organization built homes in Texas, Mississippi, Louisiana, and Alabama in the twelve months following Hurricanes Katrina and Rita.

In May 2010, to coincide with Oprah's show coming off air, Oprah's Angel Network stopped taking donations and was wound up.

In 2004, Winfrey became the first black person to hit the 50 most generous Americans chart, an honor she held until 2010. By 2012, she had donated around $400 million to educational causes. In addition, she had awarded over 400 scholarships to Morehouse College in Atlanta, Georgia. As a result of her generosity, Winfrey was awarded the first Bob Hope Humanitarian Award at the 2002 Emmy Awards for her service to television and film. In 2013, then-President Barack Obama awarded Winfrey the Presidential Medal of Freedom.

Winfrey became famous for giving away expensive gifts to the live audiences at her shows, but she was just as generous to her staff. To celebrate twenty years on national television and as a gesture of thanks to her employees for all their hard work, Winfrey took her entire team and their families on vacation to Hawaii in 2006, just over 1,000 people in total.

In 2004, Winfrey filmed an episode of her show, *Oprah's Christmas Kindness,* in South Africa. She wanted to raise awareness of the impact of poverty and AIDS on young children. Over the course of 21 days, Winfrey and her team visited several schools and orphanages in deprived areas, giving out Christmas presents to 50,000 children, including dolls, soccer balls, and school supplies. Throughout the show, Winfrey called for viewers to donate money to Oprah's Angel Network, raising over $7,000,000.

Winfrey invested $40 million in establishing the Oprah Winfrey Leadership Academy for Girls in Henley on Klip, South Africa. The school opened in January 2007, opening its doors to an initial 150 pupils, which eventually became 450. The Academy had state-of-the-art classrooms, computer and science laboratories, a well-stocked library, theater, and even a yoga studio and beauty salon. Winfrey won praise from Nelson Mandela for leaving her own difficult past behind to help others, but there were some who criticized the school for being elitist and inappropriately luxurious. Winfrey countered the complaints by saying, "If you are surrounded by beautiful things and wonderful teachers who inspire you, that beauty brings out the beauty in you."

However, all Winfrey's good intentions were overshadowed when, a few months later, a dorm matron was arrested following accusations of sexual abuse against several seventh and eighth graders. By all accounts, Winfrey was devastated, accusing the school staff of covering up what had happened. She immediately dismissed the principal and vowed to eliminate any other problem staff. Unfortunately, less than two years later, before the dorm matron had even faced trial, a number of girls were suspended or expelled following claims that they had attempted to force other students into romantic and sexual relationships.

Things quickly fell apart. *The Guardian* reported in the following year that Oprah had come to an agreement with the principal, who had accused her of defamation in claiming that she had been aware of the dorm matron's actions. In addition, the dorm matron was soon after acquitted of all charges after a judge ruled the girls' stories contradictory and not credible.

Speaking to the press, the matron said that her life had been ruined. Following her dismissal from the Academy, she was out of money, out of work, and felt that she may never forgive Winfrey, who continued to support the girls who had made the allegations.

Despite its bumpy start, the Academy is still welcoming girls through its doors, recently celebrating its 10th anniversary.

The Academy scandal may be part of the reason why Oprah was recently caught up in another child abuse scandal. During the Covid-19 pandemic, false rumors spread online like wildfire, accusing the media mogul of sex trafficking and claiming that the police had raided her Florida home. A number of tweets made these allegations, believed to have been inspired by the right-wing conspiracy, QAnon. Many of the tweets pointed to Winfrey's friendship with disgraced film producer Harvey Weinstein, who had recently been sentenced to 23 years for rape. Some claimed that Winfrey was just one of many celebrities, including Tom Hanks and Ellen DeGeneres, who had been arrested for sex offenses, with the global pandemic a cover to enable their arrests.

Winfrey had been criticized for her friendship with Weinstein when news broke of his predatory behavior. Many claimed that his actions were an open secret, meaning that Winfrey would have been fully aware of allegations against him, yet was very happy to socialize with the producer. Although Winfrey was quick to condemn Weinstein's "hideous behavior" once he was charged, a spokesman was forced to issue a denial after TMZ reported that Winfrey had encouraged Weinstein to defend himself against allegations of misconduct. On top of that, actress Kadian Noble reported that Weinstein had introduced her to Winfrey and Naomi Campbell as part of a bid to seduce her, giving rise to lurid headlines stating, "Weinstein used Oprah and Naomi to seduce me."

Following the tweets, Winfrey tweeted herself, writing, "Just got a phone call that my name is trending. And being trolled for some awful FAKE thing. It's NOT TRUE. Haven't been raided, or arrested. Just sanitizing and self-distancing with the rest of the world. Stay safe everybody."

Director Ava DuVernay also weighed in, tweeting, "Trolls + bots began this disgusting rumor. Mean-spirited minds kept it going. Oprah has worked for decades on behalf of others.

Given hundreds of millions to individuals + causes in need. Shared her own abuse as a child to help folks heal. Shame on all who participated in this."

Chapter 8

Legacy

"Do the one thing you think you cannot do. Fail at it. Try again. Do better the second time. The only people who never tumble are those who never mount the high wire."

CNN and Time.com described Winfrey as "arguably the world's most powerful woman, while *The American Spectator* named her as "one of the 100 people who most influenced the 20th Century". In addition, Winfrey is the only person ever to have appeared on *TIME's* list of most influential people ten different times.

These are by no means the only publications and organizations which have described Winfrey in these types of terms. *Life, USA Today, Ladies Home Journal, Entertainment Weekly,* and *Forbes* have all awarded her similar accolades, with *Life* listing Winfrey alongside such names as Jesus Christ and Elvis Presley as one of 100 people who changed the world. Columnist

Maureen Dowd said of Winfrey, "She is the top alpha female in this country. She has more credibility than the president. Other successful women, such as Hillary Clinton and Martha Stewart, had to be publicly slapped down before they could move forward. Even Condi has had to play the protégé with Bush. None of this happened to Oprah – she is a straight-ahead success story." Perhaps this is why Winfrey has captured the public imagination so successfully. She is the epitome of the American dream, an African-American woman who suffered a horrific childhood to rise to the pinnacle of success by dint of hard work and talent.

If Winfrey can make it, anyone can.

So unique and enduring has been Winfrey's style that *The Wall Street Journal* created the term 'Oprahfication' to denote her peculiar type of public confession as a vehicle for therapy. *Time* described her style as "rapport talk" instead of the "report talk" of the likes of Phil Donahue. Oprah did not just interview her guests for their stories; she shared her own, empathizing with them, discussing her struggles with weight, romantic difficulties, her abusive past, many times unable to keep herself from crying with her guests. As *Time* put it, "She makes people care because she cares. That is Winfrey's genius and will be her legacy, as the changes she has wrought in the talk show continue to permeate our culture and shape our lives."

Oprahfication has even expanded into politics, with Bill Clinton credited as the first politician who drew inspiration from her style to build a connection with voters. *Newsweek* wrote, "Every time a politician lets his lip quiver or a cable anchor 'emotes' on TV, they nod to the cult of confession that Oprah helped create."

Winfrey did not just influence politicians; she had an impact on voters too. She publicly endorsed Barack Obama in the 2008 presidential election, the first time she had come out in support of a candidate. She held a fundraiser for Obama at her Santa Barbara estate and joined him on several rallies. The Columbia, South Carolina event on December 9, 2007, pulled in almost 30,000 attendees, the largest for any political event that year.

Economists at the University of Maryland, College Park, analyzed voting patterns and concluded that Winfrey's support of Obama had won him anywhere between 420,000 and 1,600,000 votes in the Democratic primaries, suggesting that Winfrey had tipped the balance in favor of Obama over Hillary Clinton. It was said that Rod Blagojevich, governor of Illinois, was so impressed by Winfrey's performance that he was tempted to offer Winfrey Obama's vacant senate seat, saying she had been the most critical person in Obama's election, with "a voice larger than all 100 senators combined." However, Winfrey made it clear that she had no interest in entering politics.

Winfrey has had an impact on the world of spirituality as well. In 2002, *Christianity Today* published a piece entitled "The Church of O," which discussed how Winfrey had been established as an influential spiritual leader. The article stated that "Since 1994 when she abandoned traditional talk-show fare for more edifying content, and 1998 when she began 'Change Your Life TV,' Oprah's most significant role has become that of a spiritual leader. To her audience of more than 22 million mostly female viewers, she has become a postmodern priestess—an icon of church-free spirituality."

Since the mid-1990s, *The Oprah Winfrey Show* had a strong focus on uplifting and altruistic subjects, inspiring many to become actively involved in charity. A study carried out by scientists at the Universities of Cambridge, Plymouth, and California showed that watching a positive clip from *The Oprah Winfrey Show* influenced subjects to be twice as helpful as those shown in a British comedy or nature documentary.

While appearing on *The Oprah Winfrey Show,* Roseanne Barr told Winfrey, "you're the African Mother Goddess of us all," a remark that was met with a great deal of support from the studio audience. It certainly appears to be true that Winfrey has managed to capture a unique place in the hearts and minds of many Americans (and indeed, people across the globe). Not only is her personal story truly inspirational, but she also practices what she preaches, choosing to actively put her money and time towards those things she deems appropriate rather than simply paying lip service to the notion of charity.

At the time of writing, Winfrey is 67 years of age and shows no sign of slowing down. She continues to innovate and pursue new ventures, always looking for new challenges and ways of making a positive impact on the world.

In a quote inspired by the teachings of *The Secret,* Winfrey said, "The key to realizing a dream is to focus not on success but on significance — and then even the small steps and little victories along your path will take on greater meaning." This philosophy certainly seems to have brought Winfrey everything she could have dreamed of and more.

Made in United States
Troutdale, OR
09/11/2024